# 'TWAS IN THE MOON OF WINTERTIME

# 'TWAS IN THE MOON OF WINTERTIME

## The First American Christmas Carol

adapted by Roz Abisch     illustrated by Boche Kaplan

Prentice-Hall, Inc.   Englewood Cliffs, N.J.

'TWAS IN THE MOON OF WINTERTIME adapted by Roz Abisch  Illustrated by Boche Kaplan  © 1969 by Roz Abisch and Boche Kaplan  All rights reserved. No part of this book may be reproduced in any form or by any means, except for the inclusion of brief quotations in a review, without permission in writing from the publisher.  13-933358-4  Library of Congress Catalog Card Number: 69-12825  Printed in the United States of America • J

 for Jean E. Reynolds

In the wild north country of the New World, in the land of forests and lakes, there lived a great Indian tribe called the Hurons.

These people of the north woods thought the world rested upon the back of a very large turtle. They believed that the sun disappeared each night into a tunnel in the earth, only to rise from the other end next morning.

To keep them safe from harm and evil, the 🪶 Hurons made charms out of 🦷 beavers' teeth and 🐟 fish bones, out of odd-shaped pebbles and splinters of wood. Their god was a Great Spirit who lived in the ☁ sky. He was known to them as Gitchi Manitou. And he watched over forests and lakes and man and beast alike.

Into this new land of 🏹 hunters and 🐎 warriors, into this place of 🐴 strange spirits and ⊕ charms, came a French ✝ Jesuit missionary by the name of Jean de Brébeuf. Father Jean lived with the 🪶 Hurons and learned their language and customs. They welcomed him into their lodges 🛖 as a nephew to the old people, a faithful brother to those of his own age, and an uncle to the children.

Father Jean hoped to
lead the sons of the

...forest to the teachings of the gentle Master. In their own language, he told them the story of the ✝ cross. And there, in the woodlands of the north, he spoke of that night of nights— when long ago Jesus was born...

'Twas in the moon of wintertime
when all the birds had fled,

That mighty Gitchi Manitou
    sent angel choirs instead.

Before their light the stars grew dim,
And wandering hunters heard the hymn—
"Jesus, your King, is born. Jesus is born."

Within a lodge of broken bark
  the tender Babe was found,
A ragged robe of rabbit skin
  enwrapped His beauty round.

And as the hunter braves drew near,
The angel song rang loud and clear—
"Jesus, your King, is born. Jesus is born."

The earliest moon of wintertime
is not so round and fair,
As was the ring of glory
on the helpless Infant there.

While chiefs from far before Him knelt,
With gifts of fox and beaver pelt—
"Jesus, your King is born. Jesus is born."

O children of the forest free,
O sons of Manitou,
The Holy Child of earth and Heaven
is born today for you.

Come kneel before the radiant Boy
Who brings you beauty, peace, and joy—
"Jesus, your King, is born, Jesus is born."

# 'TWAS IN THE MOON

Original words in Huron Indian
by Father Jean de Brébeuf, 1593–1649
English Translation: J.E. Middleton

Traditional French [WE]

*Andante*

1. 'Twas in the moon of win-ter-time when all the birds had
2. With-in a lodge of bro-ken bark the ten-der Babe was
3. The ear-liest moon of win-ter time is not so round and
4. O chil-dren of the for-est free, O sons of Man-i-

Es - ten—ni—a—lon de tson - ue I e - sus Ahaton —

fled,    That might-y Git-chi Man-i-tou sent
found,   A rag-ged robe of rab-bit skin en-
fair,    As was the ring of glo-ry on the
tou,     The Ho-ly Child of earth and Heav'n is

nia,    On - nau - a - te - ua 'd'o - ki n'on - an —

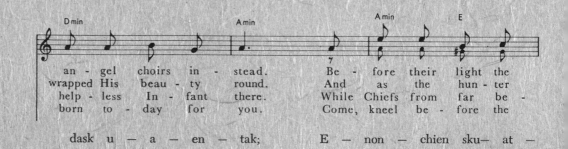

an - gel choirs in - stead.    Be - fore their light the
wrapped His beau-ty round.    And as the hun-ter
help-less In - fant there.    While Chiefs from far be-
born to - day for you.    Come, kneel be - fore the

dask u - a - en — tak;    E — non — chien sku— at —

# OF WINTERTIME

Translation and arrangement from THE INTERNATIONAL BOOK OF CHRISTMAS CAROLS by Walter Ehret and George K. Evans, Prentice-Hall, Inc. and Walton Music Corporation, 1963.

stars grew dim, And wan-d'ring hun-ters heard the hymn:___
braves drew nigh, The an-gel song rang loud and high:___
fore him knelt, With gifts of fox and bea-ver pelt.___
ra-diant Boy Who brings you beau-ty, peace and joy.___

ri — ho — tat n'on — u — an — dil — on — rac — hat — ha.

**REFRAIN**

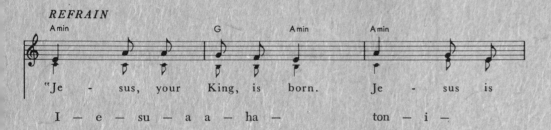

"Je - sus, your King, is born. Je - sus is

I — e — su — a — a — ha — ton — i —

born. *In ex - cel - sis glo - ri - a!"*

a .

## Note:

Father Jean de Brébeuf (1593-1649)

Jean de Brébeuf established the first Jesuit mission for the Huron Indians on Georgian Bay in Canada. In the early 1640's, Father Brébeuf wrote 'TWAS IN THE MOON OF WINTERTIME, and set it to the tune of an old French folk song. It was written especially for the Hurons among whom he lived and worked, and it is said to be the first Christmas carol produced in the New World.